This book is written by

_____

© 2019 Pretty Laks Press

All Rights Reserved

Book Layout, Illustration © Pretty Laks Press

No part of this book may be reproduced, scanned or distributed in any printed or electronic form without prior permission from the author.

You are good at

_____

You always help me to

_____

I love when
you cook

_____

You are smarter than

_____

My favorite thing about you is

_____

If I had million bucks I would buy you

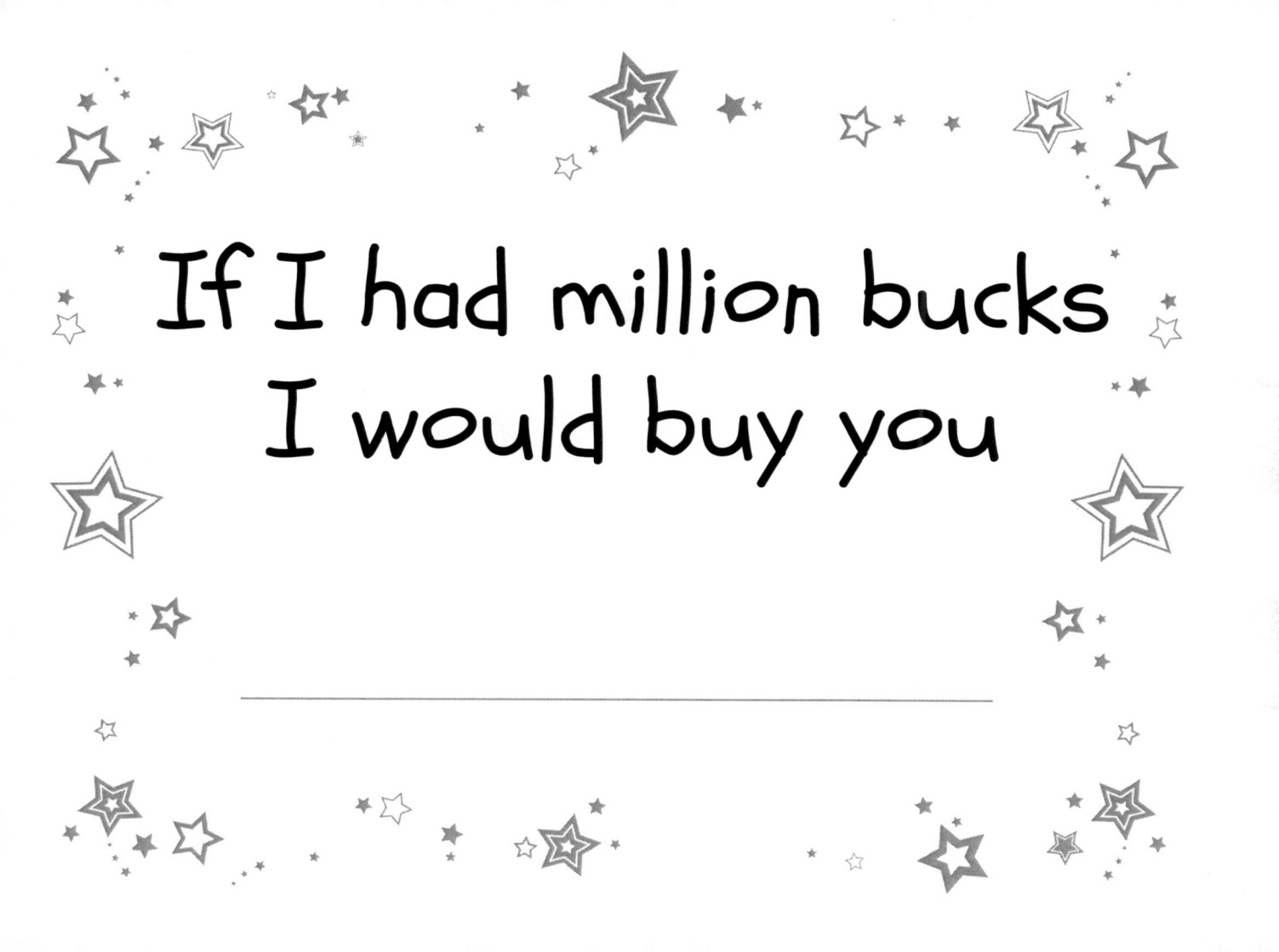

_____

I like when you call me

_____

Our favorite thing to do together is

_____

You are the happiest when

_____

Your favorite food is

_____

Tv show/movie that we both love is

_____

You are stronger than

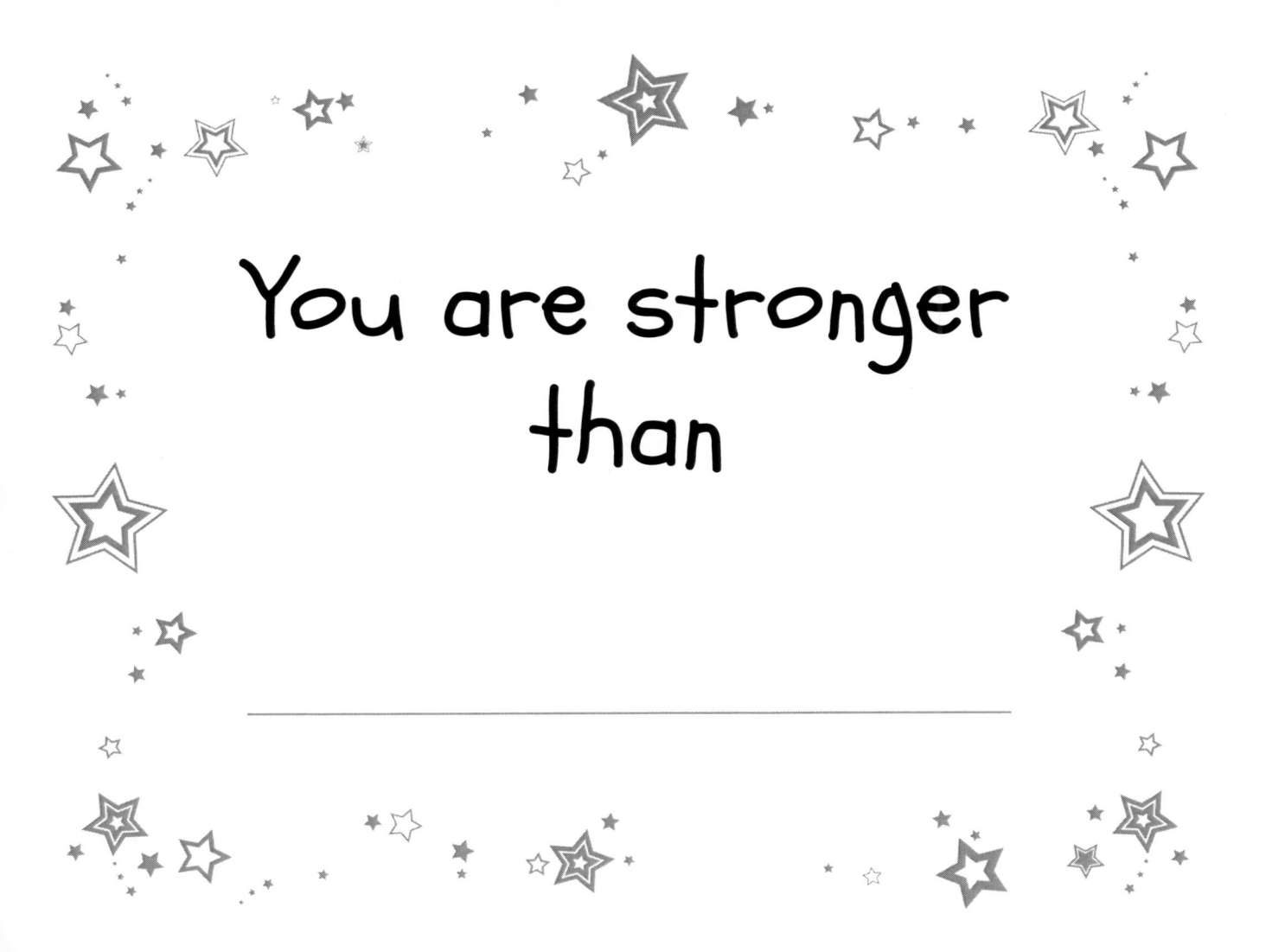

_____

You are special to me because

_____

You make everyone

_____

You taught me how to

_____

I love when you tell stories about

_____

You inspire me to do

_____

I enjoyed a lot when we went to

_____

I love when we prank

_____

I love you a lot because you never

_____

Funniest thing you do is

_____

I wish we have more time to

_____

I feel safe when you

_____

You don't care about

_____

I like when you make funny

_____

I loved when you surprised me with

_____

I love you more than

_____

Game I like to play with you is

_____

You are proud of me when I

_____

I want you to know that I will

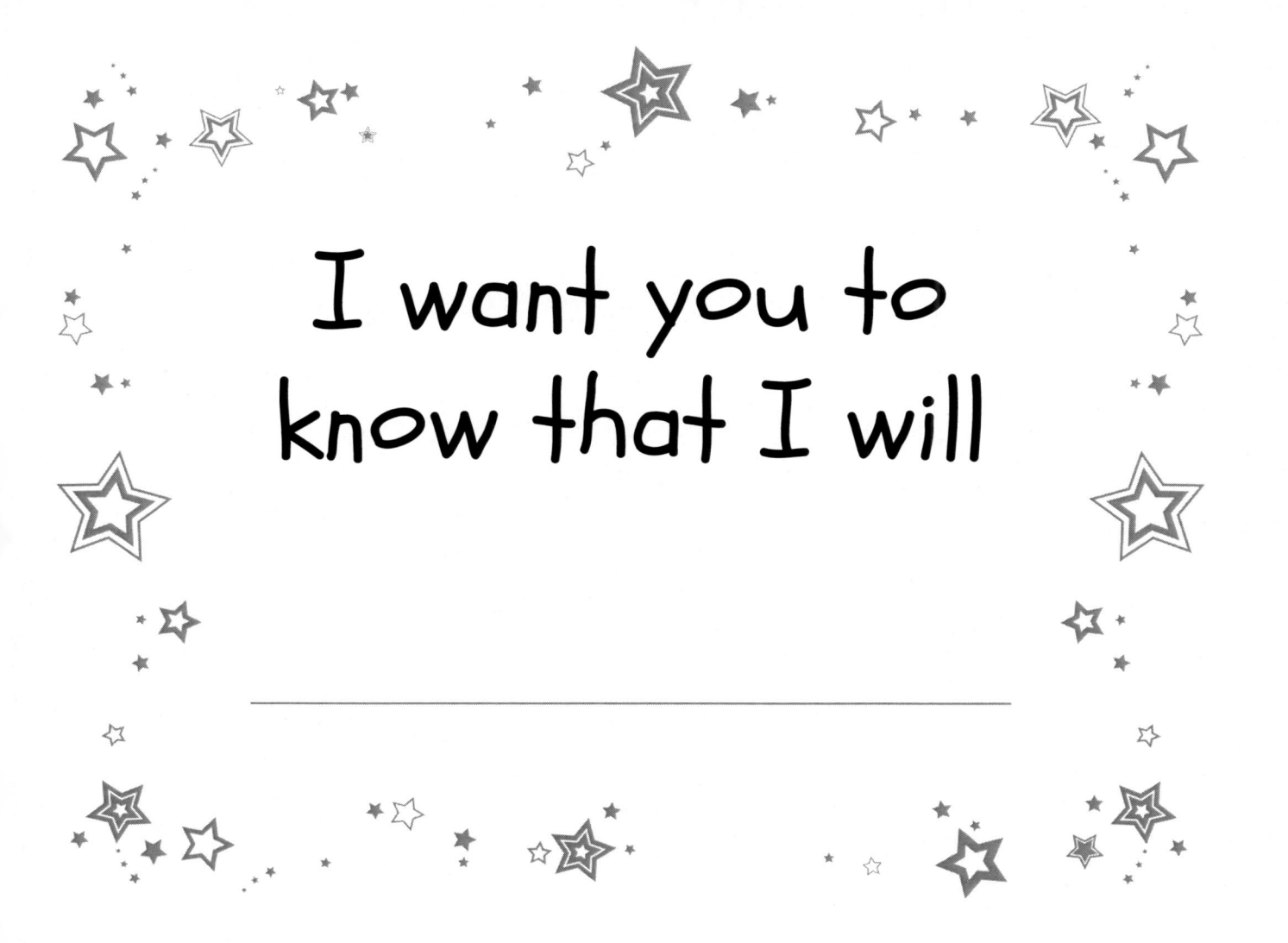

_____

Made in United States
North Haven, CT
24 April 2024